Centre for Educational Research and Innovation (CERI)

INNOVATION IN IN-SERVICE EDUCATION AND TRAINING OF TEACHERS

Practice and Theory

ORGANISATION FOR ECONOMIC CO-OPERATION AND DEVELOPMENT

1978

The Organisation for Economic Co-operation and Development (OECD) was set up under a Convention signed in Paris on 14th December 1960, which provides that the OECD shall promote policies designed:
— to achieve the highest sustainable economic growth and employment and a rising standard of living in Member countries, while maintaining financial stability, and thus to contribute to the development of the world economy;
— to contribute to sound economic expansion in Member as well as non-member countries in the process of economic development;
— to contribute to the expansion of world trade on a multilateral, non-discriminatory basis in accordance with international obligations.

The Members of OECD are Australia, Austria, Belgium, Canada, Denmark, Finland, France, the Federal Republic of Germany, Greece, Iceland, Ireland, Italy, Japan, Luxembourg, the Netherlands, New Zealand, Norway, Portugal, Spain, Sweden, Switzerland, Turkey, the United Kingdom and the United States.

The Centre for Educational Research and Innovation was created in June 1968 by the Council of the Organisation for Economic Co-operation and Development for an initial period of three years, with the help of grants from the Ford Foundation and the Royal Dutch Shell Group of Companies. In May 1971, the Council decided that the Centre should continue its work for a period of five years as from 1st January 1972. In July 1976 it extended this mandate for the following five years, 1977-82.

The main objectives of the Centre are as follows:
— *to promote and support the development of research activities in education and undertake such research activities where appropriate;*
— *to promote and support pilot experiments with a view to introducing and testing innovations in the educational system;*
— *to promote the development of co-operation between Member countries in the field of educational research and innovation.*

The Centre functions within the Organisation for Economic Co-operation and Development in accordance with the decisions of the Council of the Organisation, under the authority of the Secretary-General. It is supervised by a Governing Board composed of one national expert in its field of competence from each of the countries participating in its programme of work.

The opinions expressed and arguments employed in this publication
are the responsibility of the author
and do not necessarily represent those of the OECD.

© OECD, 1978
Queries concerning permissions or translation rights should be addressed to:
Director of Information, OECD
2, rue André-Pascal, 75775 PARIS CEDEX 16, France.

CONTENTS

Preface 5

I. Introduction 7

II. National Contextual Factors 11

III. Users: Individual and System Needs 21

IV. Tasks: Policies and Programmes 25

V. Resources: Providing Agents and Agencies 29

VI. Strategies and Methods: Governance, Training, Evaluation and Dissemination 33

VII. Some Interim Conclusions 45

Appendices

1. Bibliography 53
   A. National Reports 53
   B. Selective Bibliography 54

2. The Case Studies 59

3. A Provisional Conceptual Framework 61

PREFACE

A great part of the OECD work on innovation in education focused on the complex factors relating to the means which the school has at its disposal for its self renewal. For example, the studies and analyses undertaken in the framework of the CERI programme on the Creativity of the School or those of the programme of the Education Committee on Teacher Policies, have underscored the great role attached to the In-service Education and Training (INSET) needs of the teachers, as one of the key factors affecting educational change. As part of the on-going programme of CERI, it was therefore decided to give special attention to an analysis of this particular topic in the context of educational innovation policies and theories as they emerge within Member countries.

It was agreed at the outset of this work that broad dissemination of national practices and experience in this field was necessary, because of the present weakness of the comparative analyses at international level. That is why the project started with the preparation of a series of national monographs, already published by the Centre; the list of these monographs is given in Appendix 1 and their detailed content in Appendix 2. The report below, concluding the first phase of the work, presents a synthesis of the results of this survey of country experience and of an international seminar at which innovative practices of INSET were reviewed, in an attempt to place them within a provisional conceptual framework.

The first phase of the work also provided an opportunity to define priorities for further studies which are now being undertaken in the framework of the second phase of the project. These are as follows:

i) the contribution of adult learning theories and practices to INSET;
ii) the role of school-focused training;
iii) evaluation of INSET;
iv) new INSET materials;
v) role and training of teacher trainers;
vi) INSET finance and resources.

It should be noted that the United States authorities have shown a special interest in this project which materialised in a grant from the National Institute of Education to the Centre; this has enabled the work to proceed at a level and depth which otherwise would not have been possible. The General Report hereafter, prepared by Dr. R. Bolam, School of Education, University of Bristol, United Kingdom, must be considered as an interim report concluding the first phase of information and clarification of the issues. It will be followed, at the end of the second phase of the work, by a final report which would aim at providing a clear analytical basis for the continuing discussions in Member countries on the elaboration and implementation of policies in this field.

I

INTRODUCTION

This report has four principal aims. First it aims to summarize and synthesise the main findings from the first phase of a project on innovative approach to the in-service education and training (INSET) of teachers. Second, it aims to identify some of the key policy issues which emerge from this first phase. Third, it aims to explore the utility of certain theoretical ideas by rooting the synthesis in a provisional conceptual framework for continuing professional development in education. Fourth, it aims to identify ways in which OECD might usefully contribute to future work in the field of INSET.

At the outset of the project, in 1975, one thing was very clear: informed professional opinion in several OECD Member countries was virtually unanimous in recommending that a very high priority should be given to the expansion and improvement of in-service training as an investment in the future quality of the teaching force. This agreement about the importance of INSET had given rise in several Member countries to a detailed consideration of necessary changes in its nature, scale, costs, organisation and structure.

Certain major and recurring issues were identifiable. One was that of striking the right balance between the concern of individual teachers and their professional associations for professional and career development, the concern of employers for the needs of pupils and schools and the concern of INSET providing institutions for academic excellence and autonomy. A second was that of creating appropriate and effective linkage and co-ordination between schools and the various external INSET support agencies on the one hand and between the external agencies themselves on the other hand. A third was that of redefining the roles of existing INSET agencies and of creating innovative institutions where these are necessary. A fourth was that of devising new strategies - for example, school-based training - to meet the commonly expressed demand for practical and relevant INSET. A fifth and fundamentally important issue was that of ensuring that the approach to INSET at national, regional and local levels is cost-effective in terms of teacher release and replacement, the rational use of resources and the improvement of the educational system.

These, and other similar, problems were being tackled in a variety of ways by OECD Member countries and a number of significant and potentially adaptable approaches had been devised. It was, therefore, an opportune time to study and report on such developments so that information and experience of a practical kind could be widely disseminated amongst Member countries.

It was against this background that the US National Institute of Education (NIE) and the OECD agreed to sponsor jointly an international project on innovative approaches to INSET. Reports were commissioned from leading teacher educators in the following countries: Australia; Canada; France; Germany and Switzerland; Japan; the Netherlands; Sweden; United Kingdom; United States. A post-seminar contribution from Italy has been added. (See Appendices for details. It is important to note that these reports were not official statements of national policy.) Each report contained an outline of the national context and the main features of INSET; several intensive case-studies of innovative approaches to INSET; conclusions on the implications of the case-studies for the future of INSET. These national reports were discussed at an international seminar on the In-Service Education and Training (INSET) of Teachers which was held in Philadelphia, Pennsylvania from June 27th to July 3rd, 1976. It, too, was sponsored jointly by NIE and OECD and was hosted by Research for Better Schools Inc.

Over 70 participants from ten countries attended the Philadelphia seminar. The two principal aims of the seminar were:

a) To identify, describe and critically analyse some major, significant and potentially adaptable INSET practices in ten OECD Member countries.
b) To disseminate the findings in such a way that Member countries can decide whether or not these practices are relevant and adaptable to their own national systems.

The four dominant seminar themes were:

a) Rationale and philosophy.
b) Content and structure.
c) Practices and methods of providing INSET.
d) Evaluation, generalisability and adaptability.

Each theme was introduced in a key-note exposition and was then explored and discussed in small group meetings, panel presentations and plenary group meetings. A notable and effective feature of the seminar was the daily Steering Committee meetings which were open to all participants. These provided immediate, formative evaluation about progress and made for a dynamic and flexible programme which was thus very responsive to the expressed wishes of the participants – an extremely important factor in a five-day international conference.

The rest of this synthesis report is organised on the basis of the analytic framework presented in Appendix 3. Thus, the next Section outlines some of the main national contextual variables which affect

INSET in the participating countries. Section III analyses the characteristics and needs of the 'users' of INSET - teachers, schools and school systems. Section IV identifies two main types of task in INSET - the formulation of policy and programmes - and analyses them at four main levels: national, regional/state, local and institutional. Section V analyses the characteristics of INSET providing agents and agencies and Section VI analyses some of their principal strategies and methods. Finally, Section VII draws some conclusions from the report.

II

NATIONAL CONTEXTUAL FACTORS

The national reports outlined the contextual factors bearing upon developments and innovations in INSET in each country. Earlier OECD reports had also dealt with relevant contextual factors, but in much greater detail. One report on Teacher Policies (OECD, 1976), for example, summarises current trends and issues under four broad headings:

- the changing context of the professional activity of teaching;
- changes in working conditions and needs for teachers;
- new standards for teacher education;
- consequences for costs and planning.

The pre-seminar reports provided striking confirmation of the growing importance of INSET (e.g. A 22, F 5, GS 17, J 18, UK 1, US 66)*. The seminar itself provided three main reasons for this trend: first, it is inherently important that teachers, of all people, should continue with their personal and professional education; second, the rapid, extensive and fundamental nature of present-day change – technological, economic, cultural, social, political – makes it imperative for the education system in general and teachers in particular to review and modify teaching methods and curricula; third, for widely prevalent demographic reasons, the demand for new teachers is dropping sharply and the INSET needs of a stable teaching force become especially important.

For these and other reasons, several countries have made moves to establish or rationalise planning and organisational arrangements for INSET. Sweden already has comprehensive machinery (S 15) and articulated systems are described in the German (GS 11) and Japanese (J 18) reports. The Netherlands (N 13) is moving out of an unplanned phase, as also are England and Wales (UK 12) and France (F 5). Swiss teachers are also said to be demanding a planned national system (GS 22). Australia's Teacher Development Programme is described (A 41) and although the economic situation has recently deteriorated, appears to

---

* Page references to the reports use the following abbreviations:
A: Australia; I: Italy; UK: United Kingdom; C: Canada; J: Japan; US: United States; F: France; N: Netherlands; GS: Germany and Switzerland; S: Sweden;

have been given exceptional financial support. In the USA the National Advisory Council on Education Professions Development has recommended a more extensive and co-ordinated policy (US 120), presumably because of what Rubin refers to as the 'conspicuous absence of systematisation' (US 15).

These trends towards rationalisation have to some extent been stimulated by economic recession but a more fundamental thrust appears to have come from a felt need to co-ordinate the hitherto unplanned growth of INSET within a national policy framework which takes comprehensive account of the available resources, including a variety of institutions of higher education. The Swedish report puts it as follows:

> "But the experience of INSET gained in Sweden since the beginning of the 1950s shows quite plainly that rules and regulations are needed. Nor is post-initial education at grass-roots enough. There must be a collective, overall policy to which local measures can be related."
> (S 9).

The Canadian report (C 8) refers to "an astonishing amount of internal INSET through a variety of mechanisms" and points out that little is known about is impact and effectiveness. The United States report lists the types and numbers of teacher educators involved in INSET and remarks upon the considerable 'extent and complexity of in-service organisations' (US 146). The situation in France is characterised in similar terms (F 5).

However, although there is widespread agreement in Member countries about the importance of INSET, although better planning procedures are being adopted and although a great deal of INSET is already going on, there is much less clarity and agreement about the precise nature and aims of INSET. Although several definitions of INSET were offered in the reports (S 13, GS 71, US 17 and 143), these frequently varied in scope, and it soon became evident that some seminar participants, sometimes from the same country, were using the term INSET in different ways from each other. This problem was recognised at the outset when Dr. Malcolm Skilbeck, in introducing the theme, identified a major task as the definition and de-limitation of the field. Skilbeck argued that INSET includes a whole range of components and aims, viz: updating teacher skills and knowledge but with no change of role; preparation for new roles and positions; improvement in qualification and status; external or internal (i.e. school) provision; a focus on strictly practical or on wider educational needs; programme availability throughout teachers' careers - such programmes to include those lasting two hours and those lasting several years.

This helped to clarify the two principal definitions of INSET, which we may label "narrow" and "broad", which were implicit in contributions to the seminar. The "narrow" definition is exemplified in one quoted in the American report (US 72):

> "... employment-oriented education... activities which have as their intended purpose preparation for specific program demands which decisions within the system have created..."

The "broad" definition is offered in the same report (US 71):

> "Every teacher is also a career-long student. That portion of his education which follows in time, (1) his initial certification and (2) employment, is known as in-service teacher education."

By implication, this "broad" definition encompasses theoretical work at doctoral and master's levels, as well as the two-hour evening workshop of a strictly practical nature.

The broad definition provides a useful theoretical basis for devising a typology which encompasses all aspects of INSET. Howey quotes several attempts to formulate typologies "in terms of design, governance and support". He himself distinguishes between "seven categories of in-service:

1. transitional;
2. school renewal/role re-orientation;
3. context specific/role improvements;
4. personal growth;
5. continuing formal education;
6. professional development; and
7. career progression".

Howey also summarises Joyce's, 1976, typology of forms or contexts of INSET: job-embedded; job-related; credential-oriented; professional organisation-related; and self-directed (US 72-73).

But from a policy-making standpoint, the "broad" definition certainly presents some practical problems. For example, it makes sense to distinguish between up-dating the knowledge and skills needed for a teacher's present job, from the further training needed to prepare him for a new job (e.g. a principalship). At present, countries differ as to whether the latter can legitimately be regarded as INSET.

A working committee established by the Swedish National Board of Education distinguished between five types of INSET (S 14):

> <u>INSET 1</u>: INSET whose content is co-ordinated with basic training. There are components of basic training which demand amplification via INSET after the teachers have acquired a certain measure of professional experience.
>
> <u>INSET 2</u>: INSET of locally determined content. Within the individual school of municipality, groups or individuals, whether they belong to the school management, the teaching staff or other personnel categories, observe INSET requirements which may often be peculiar to their school or school system.

INSET 3: INSET of centrally and regionally determined content. Central and regional authorities are capable of the continuous surveillance of INSET requirements, e.g. in connection with their work on school evaluation, curricular development and research and development activities.

INSET 4: INSET whose content is determined by educational reforms or by thoroughgoing curricular revisions. Reforms or changes of this kind often necessitate special INSET measures.

INSET 5: INSET whose content is determined by specific individual needs."

In England a similar classification has also been produced by a national committee (UK 8-11). The UK report also contained the typology of INSET which has been adapted slightly in Table 2.1 to fit in with the dimensions of the model in Appendix 3. This typology embraces many of the categories discussed above: the source or location of the INSET providing agent; the type of strategy open to it; the location of the activity and the target users. The asterisks indicate the strategies which are likely to apply to particular target users.

As Howey points out (US 73) most of these typologies are crude and incomplete; but at least a start is now being made. However, in his seminar contribution, Dr. Karl Frey made a more fundamental point about these typologies: that they are essentially descriptive and analytic and do not, of themselves, either generate any critique of existing practice or indicate positive steps forward. The LIL model outlined in the German report (GS 80) aims to provide such a dynamic framework.

These conceptual problems are not simply theoretical ones. The American report argues (US 73) that they have important practical implications for deciding

"... how different in-service activities are to be legitimised, monitored, supported, accredited, governed and given priority.
.... more articulate conceptualisation will help defuse power struggles within systems and the different role groups within these systems."

Similar views are expressed in the French report (F 6).

Implicit in many of the definitions discussed in the various national reports is the idea that INSET should be an integral part of continuing or recurrent education. However, although this is often mentioned it is clear that, as yet, little progress has been made in achieving this goal. Perhaps the most striking illustration of this is contained in the French report. As Belbenoit says:

"(France) has made such a contribution to the concept of "permanent education" that the expression frequently appears in French in foreign texts." (F 5).

Table 2.1. A TYPOLOGY OF INSET STRATEGIES

SOURCE OF AGENT	INSET PROVISION STRATEGY OR METHOD	ON-SITE INDIVIDUAL	ON-SITE GROUP	ON-SITE WHOLE STAFF	OFF-SITE INDIVIDUAL	OFF-SITE GROUP	OFF-SITE WHOLE STAFF
Internal (i.e. school)	1. Individual teaching experience	*					
	2. Team teaching experience	*	*				
	3. Regular department/staff meetings	*	*	*			
	4. Membership of ad hoc working party (e.g. on curriculum development)	*	*	*			
	5. Resources centre training	*	*				
	6. Teacher tutor: a) counselling	*					
	b) training	*	*				
	c) group discussions		*				
	7. Study visits to other schools	*	*	*	*	*	*
	8. Study conference				*	*	*
External (e.g. teachers' centre; college of education)	1. Short course				*	*	
	2. Longer course				*		
	3. Secondment to broaden experience (e.g. to curriculum development project)	*	*				
	4. Field study research in own school	*	*	*			
	5. Reading/private study	*			*		
	6. Consultancy (e.g. with L.E.A. adviser or organisation development consultant)				*	*	*
	7. Sabbatical term				*		

He goes on:

> "The present position of INSET in France is something of a paradox. ... One might have expected to find... a coherent programme of action... on continual vocational training... In fact, there is nothing of the kind." (F 11)

The extent to which countries make it obligatory and provide release for teachers to engage in INSET activities varies. In Japan "INSET is regarded as being part of a teachers duty" (J 3). In Sweden it is the duty of teachers to attend various courses and that of the head to ensure that his staff do so (S 8), and in Western Australia "some measure of INSET is compulsory for Government Teachers" (A 29); obviously, some degree of teacher release for INSET is mandatory in both countries. In France, the programme for primary teachers established the "revolutionary" principle of entitlement, with release, to INSET (F 20). The importance of release from teaching as an incentive to attend INSET cannot be over-stressed. In the seminar one American teacher union representative rated it above salary and university credit as a motivator.

Frequent mention is also made in the reports of another major national contextual variable - the links between initial and in-service training. There is apparently widespread agreement about the desirability of a well planned and articulated continuum - the UK report refers to the triple-I continuum of initial, induction and in-service training (UK 2) - but once again actual achievements are less impressive. Linkage between the two principal stages in teacher training - initial and in-service - is generally nominal or weak in most countries. One exception is the Swedish system of regional planning conferences for initial and in-service trainers (S 19). Another is the attempt in the UK to create a linkage role (the professional tutor) in the schools and the allocation of 20 per cent of staff time in initial training institutions to INSET (UK 36). The implications of this weak linkage for the problem associated with the transition from traineed to full-time teacher are stressed in the context of induction in two reports (UK 22, A 108) and of internship in another (US 94).

Nevertheless, in spite of these conceptual and practical difficulties, it is at least possible to apply the model outlined in Appendix 3 to the national context in a reasonably valid and helpful way. Tables 2.1a and b distinguish between two principal tasks in INSET: those related to overall structure and policy and those related to the implementation of specific programmes and courses. In most of the national reports, the planning of INSET policy and structure can be analysed at four levels - national, regional/state, local and institutional. The principal people or groups in the INSET "agency" (Column A) are usually three: someone with policy-making power; administrators or executors of that policy; and professionals who advise on policy. The INSET policy task itself (Column B) can be broken down into eight main parts:

aims, the identifications of broad content areas, finance, logistics, organisational -making machinery, research and development work, evaluation of outcomes, and dissemination throughout the system. The INSET users (Column C) include all those in the system likely to "use" INSET. A similar analysis is displayed in Table 2.1b for programme implementation. It should be noted that the individual professional is included as a major INSET provider for him or herself.

Table 2.1a. GENERAL SYSTEM POLICY AND STRUCTURE: LEVELS AND COMPONENTS

LEVEL/SYSTEM	A. INSET AGENT	B. INSET TASK	C. INSET USER
1. National	Minister + Administrators + Professionals (e.g. Inspectorate)	National INSET Policy/ Structure Aims; finance; logistics; machinery; broad content; research; evaluation; dissemination.	The National System Regional/state systems; Local systems; Providing agencies; Professional associations; Institutions (e.g. schools) Individuals (e.g. teachers)
2. Regional/State	Director + Administrators + Professionals	Regional/State INSET Policy/Structure Aims; finance; logistics; machinery; broad content; research; evaluation; dissemination.	The Regional System Local systems; Providing agencies; Professional associations; Institutions (e.g. schools) Individuals (e.g. teachers)
3. Local	Director/Superintendent + Administrators + Professionals (e.g. Inspectorate)	Local INSET Policy/ Structure Aims; finance; logistics; machinery; broad content; research; evaluation; dissemination.	The Local System Providing agencies; Professional associations; Institutions (e.g. schools) Individuals (e.g. teachers)
4. Institution (e.g. school)	Head/Principal + INSET Director (e.g. Professional Tutor) + Staff Committee	School INSET Policy/ Structure Aims; finance; logistics; machinery; broad content; research; evaluation; dissemination.	Institution/School System Whole staff Departments/Sections Individuals

Table 2.1b. INSET PROVIDING AGENCIES: POLICY AND PROGRAMMES

AGENCY	A. INSET AGENT	B. INSET TASK	C. INSET USER
1. External (e.g. University, Polytechnic, College, Teachers' Centre, Local inspectorate, National inspectorate, R and D Team)	Principal + INSET Director + Internal academic board	Agency Policy Aims, finance, logistics, machinery, award validation, research and evaluation Agency Programmes Detailed content and methods	Agency's Target System Local/Regional/National Systems Professional Associations Institutions (e.g. schools) Individuals (e.g. teachers)
2. Internal Institution (e.g. School)	Head/Principal + INSET Director (e.g. Professional Tutor) + Staff Committee	Policy See 4.B. Table 2.1a Programmes Content and methods	Institution/School System Whole staff Departments or Sections Individuals
3. Individual Professional	Individual professional (e.g. Teacher; Head; Administrators)	Policy Personal plans Programmes Professional training and personal education	Self Career development Personal development

III

INSET USERS: INDIVIDUAL AND SYSTEM NEEDS

In the innovation process model, the user is defined as an open system which invents an innovation or responds to an external change agent. INSET users may thus be, for example, individuals (e.g. a teacher), groups (e.g. a faculty team), institutions (e.g. a school staff), a local education authority or a national system. The characteristics and needs of these users are of crucial importance in understanding the fate of any innovation, including INSET. Relevant features of individuals include their personality and professionality; organisations may be analysed in terms of organisation theory or in terms of certain educational characteristics (Bolam, 1974).

These broad categories, and their implications for INSET needs, are confirmed in the reports. Although the terminology differs from country to country and is neither precise nor unambiguous, two major types of INSET needs, which we may call individual and system needs, are identifiable. The Swedes call these institutional and policy-based (S 93); the UK report refers to professional and system development approaches (UK 110); the Australians distinguish between teacher and employer initiated programmes (A 44). Several reports refine these distinctions: for example, the UK report refers to the INSET needs of teachers, schools, local education authorities and the national system.

In a seminar contribution, Dr. Dean Corrigan raised what was clearly a new perspective to many participants when he conceptualised the individual user of INSET as an adult learner. This immediately raises questions about the availability and relevance of adult learning theory for INSET and roots it firmly in the wider context of continuing education. Corrigan also extended the boundaries of the conceptual and practical challenge by advocating that teacher INSET should take place, at least for some of the time, alongside INSET for other "helping" professions.

Unfortunately, existing practice and knowledge about teacher INSET needs is still woefully inadequate. In the UK an attempt has been made to construct a career profile to provide a rationale for INSET but it has met with considerable opposition. Bhaerman's "continuous progress plan" may encounter a happier fate (US 115). Some progress has been made in the UK with the conceptualisation of the induction period for beginning teachers. Following earlier survey and action research projects (Taylor and Dale, 1971; Bolam, 1973) the need of beginning teachers during their first year were categorised under seven headings:

      i)   appointment and placement
     ii)   pre-service orientation
   iii)   in-service orientation
   iv)   adaptation
    v)   development
   vi)   assessment by employer
  vii)   overview of career and INSET possibilities.

This framework is now being tested out during a further action stage (UK Case 1).

The knowledge-base on the INSET needs at institutional level is even more inadequate. It is now widely recognised that innovation strategies in general and INSET strategies in particular have tended to neglect the characteristics and needs of users as social systems. Hence the great current concern for school-focused and job-embedded approaches to both innovation and INSET. However, with the exception of a small, though growing, number of case studies (e.g. Gross et al. 1971; Schmuck and Miles, 1971; Richardson, 1973), few well documented and analysed accounts of school INSET needs are reported. The potential value of school-focused INSET makes it imperative that studies should be undertaken in this field. One key question concerns the characteristics of schools (e.g. organisational climate and health) likely to affect their capacity to engage in and respond to intervention strategies of a task or process consultancy kind. Similar questions can be asked of the readiness of individuals to respond to analogous interventions like counselling, classroom observation and clinical supervision (see Section VI on strategies and methods).

One reason for its importance is that school-focused INSET acts as a powerful incentive for teachers to participate (e.g. UK 87). The more general proposition that different courses and settings vary in their attractiveness is one that has been most explored in research which asks teachers to rate courses on such criteria. Although accreditation can provide a powerful incentive, there is evidence from America that it may be counterproductive in that it does not discourage inappropriate or irrelevant courses (US 7, Vanderpool, 1975). There is some consensus amongst practitioners, however, that the major incentive for teachers to attend INSET is not a salary increase or a university credit, but release time. This was argued by an American teacher union representative and is supported by at least one national report (UK Case 1).

Even in the most de-centralised systems it is acknowledged that the needs of the local state and national systems must be taken into account alongside those of individual professionals. Recently, a national INSET committee in England and Wales stated that "Educational and social change makes new demands upon schools... (and some) ... in-service training needs result from changes originating externally, such as the reorganisation of secondary education in an area..." (UK 11), and a state-level administrator in Georgia, USA identified "required competencies", "new knowledge, practices, procedures and materials" and "the assessed needs of individual educators" as among the main sources of INSET programme content (Bottoms, 1975).

This is one reason for the greater concern now being expressed about the needs of individuals and their professional associations to participate in decisions affecting INSET. This topic is covered in more detail in Section VII but we may note here that this too is an important INSET need. On the other hand, we must also note that not all teachers apparently want to participate in decision-making procedures of this kind (Bolam, 1976).

There is general agreement in the reports about who or what actually constitutes the INSET user system, with one exception. The Australian and particularly the American reports both stress the potential outcomes of INSET for the community and the corresponding need for appropriate community representation in decisions about INSET. This stress is not evident in most of the other reports. The implications of these differences are unclear except in general terms.

Indeed this is one more example of the relative paucity of the research knowledge base concerning INSET needs at individual institutional and system levels. A substantial research effort is needed if this is to be remedied but fortunately there are encouraging signs that some initial steps are being taken (e.g. Joyce, 1976).

IV

INSET TASKS: POLICIES AND PROGRAMMES

Distinctions were made in Section II between two broad categories of INSET tasks: general system policy and structure and specific programme policy and content. Within these broad categories further distinctions are possible.

At each of the four main system levels - national, regional/state, local and institutional - the following policy management tasks can be identified:

- a) the formulation of aims;
- b) the provision of appropriate financial, logistic and decision-making resources and arrangements;
- c) the specification of broad programme content;
- d) the formulation of an accreditation policy;
- e) the evaluation of progress and outcomes of policy;
- f) the dissemination of findings throughout system;
- g) the promotion of ongoing research into system needs.

Some of the major issues associated with this broad task area are taken up below in Section VI.

Each of the three main types of providing agency in external (e.g. a teachers' centre), internal (e.g. a school) and individual professionals (e.g. a teacher) have two broad tasks. The first concerns the formulation of broad programme policy and can be analysed on similar lines to a - g above; although, of course, rather than deciding an accreditation, it is the providing agency's job to arrange for its awards to be validated. The second task concerns the formulation of an appropriate INSET programme or curriculum. This can be analysed in terms of the curriculum process model; situational analysis; goal formulation; programme building; interpretation and implementation; monitoring feedback, assessment and reconstruction (Skilbeck, 1976).

The objectives of INSET programmes vary with, of course, considerable implications for their content and structure. The most fundamental differences probably occur between courses or programmes designed to meet the two sets of needs identified above: individual and system. INSET is increasingly being seen by government at national and local levels as a means of achieving the system's policy goals. There are numerous examples of this in the reports including the first two case studies in the Netherlands report; Cases 2 and 3 in the German/ Swiss report; Case 3 in the Swedish study. INSET courses and activities designed primarily to meet individual needs do not figure prominently in the reports but the emphasis on the overseas programme in Japan (J 11, 25) and Australia (A 23) are notable exceptions.

A second obvious reason for variations in the content of courses and programmes is that the target audiences differ. Several of the case studies analyse programmes aimed at particular target groups. For example, programmes for educational administrators in Sweden (S Case 5) and England (UK 19) are described; the Australian ASTEP Project was aimed at science teachers (A Case 2); the second Netherlands case describes a counsellor training programme; beginning teachers were the particular concern of the TIPS Project (UK Case 1), and programmes aimed at training the trainers are becoming a major concern.

In introducing this theme at the seminar, Dr. Karl Frey stressed the importance of embedding practical INSET courses in an appropriate and adequate theoretical framework. All three case-studies in the German/Swiss report exemplify this approach and its final two sections elaborate on Frey's argument. However, the extent to which the content and structure of courses are based on research findings varies and some of the wider implications of this are dealt with in Section VII.3. Case 1 in the Swedish study indicates what a coherent and comprehensive policy can achieve. In Australia, most research studies have apparently been confined to identifying teachers' general INSET needs (A 33). This is broadly true, too, of England and Wales, although increasing attention is being paid to evaluating attempts to meet such needs (UK Case 1). Case 3 in the Netherlands report provides a good example of a programme based upon research by an independent organisation, in this case the Dutch Foundation for Creative Arts Education. On the other hand where the course content is primarily concerned with a curriculum subject then it is more likely to have an adequate research base; examples here include maths courses in Canada (C 16) and the Netherlands (N 63).

An increasingly common approach, apparently, is to introduce an action-research element into the programme for the participating teachers: the Ford T. project (UK 96) was designed to support classroom-based research; two of the Japaneses studies have a similar orientation (J 32; 38); similarly, two of the French studies - one of a physical education course and the other of a course designed to introduce pupil-centred approaches into the first cycle of the secondary school - included action research components.

This approach exemplifies the wider trend towards making INSET more practical and less "theoretical". One major development has been the growth of school-focused training. Another, related, move has been to involve teachers in curriculum development activities as part of INSET: the Dutch Case 4 is an example of a maths related INSET programme; the three German/Swiss case studies have this orientation; the UK report explores some of the problems of local curriculum development and INSET in a teachers' centre context (Case 4) and describes relevant work in a college (Case 2).

The conceptual problem of organising these various tasks and programme features into some form of typology is a difficult one. A useful distinction can be made between two dimensions of training: academic - pedagogic, and personal - vocational (Ferry, 1974). In the UK in particular, stress is placed upon the importance of including education as well as training at the in-service stage: hence the term in-service education and training (INSET). In all reports there was frequent mention of the importance of practical as opposed to theoretical INSET. Both of these distinctions can be accommodated in the two dimensions - and represented in a four cell diagram:

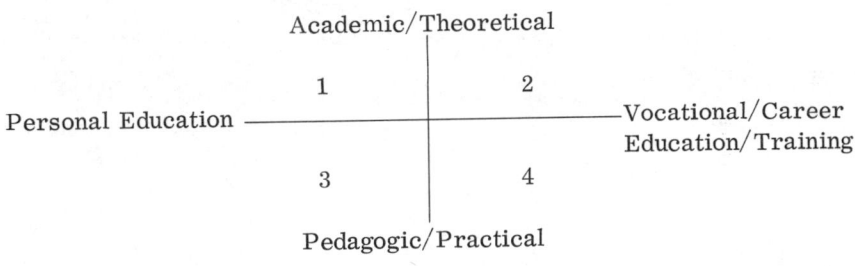

These cells may be said to represent, albeit somewhat crudely and arbitrarily, four types of INSET. How do they relate to major INSET needs? We may assume that the need of individual teachers could, in principle, be satisfied by INSET approaches within cells 1 to 4 but that national and local education authorities and employers are likely to regard types 4 and, to a lesser extent 2 and 3, as best meeting the needs of the system.

Another approach to the classification of INSET content areas is that of the Protocol materials project as described in appendix A to the article by Cruikshank, 1974. Yet another is to analyse them as innovations which are likely to provoke varying responses from the change agent and user systems depending on their perception of their relevance, relative advantage, competitive strength and feasibility (Havelock, 1969; Rogers and Shoemaker, 1971; Bolam, 1974). Thus, here too, there is clearly a great deal of research work needed before an adequate knowledge base is achieved.

V

INSET RESOURCES:
PROVIDING AGENTS AND AGENCIES

The innovation process model outlined in Appendix 3 conceptualises the change agent as an open system with internal and external characteristics. The INSET agent may be, for example, an individual lecturer or teachers' centre leader or college or education INSET department or indeed a national INSET planning board. The agent or agency may be internal to the user system (e. g. a school's professional tutor) or external to it (e. g. a curriculum project team working with a school). The agent will be perceived differently by the members of the user system according to its level, location, INSET strategies and status. The latter may be particularly important: INSET agents who are perceived as employer representatives (e. g. inspectors) may encounter difficulties in carrying out, say, a consultancy role.

Havelock's 1969 linkage role typology is very relevant to INSET: he distinguishes between nine roles: conveyor, consultant, trainer, leader, innovator, defender, knowledge-builder, practitioner and user. He recognises that they rarely exist in their pure form and that, in the real world, any one agent may play several linkage role simultaneously or sequentially. The typology is, nonetheless, useful in clarifying the linkage roles of various INSET agents.

From a practical standpoint these agents may be regarded as resources available for improving INSET. The American report estimates that 250,000 people are actual or potential INSET agents in the USA (US 66), including school principals. In England and Wales, the available INSET resource agencies are displayed in a table (UK 14) and include universities, 20 per cent of college and education staff time, polytechnics, LEA advisory teams, teachers centres and schools.

Some of the most significant innovations in the case studies deal with various new types of teacher trainers and, less frequently, with their training needs. The Swedish report describes the work and training of INSET consultants (S 15 and 30) and of study day leaders (S 46). The penultimate section of the German/Swiss report argues for university-linked practical counsellors for INSET. The role and training of school-based teacher tutors are analysed in some detail in UK Case 1. In Japan (J 38), every medium to large secondary school is said to have appointed one of its teachers as a research and training coordinator but the nature of their preparatory training is only hinted at. However, the

Milan Organisation for Teacher Training has paid particular attention to the training needs of the trainers (I 30) as did the Dutch creative arts project (N 68).

The American report (US 129) discusses the advisory role, variants of which are also mentioned in the British (UK 12) and Australian (A 16) reports. The French have developed these roles in the context of continuing education and established "integrated centres for the training of adult trainers" (F 15). However, the term "advisory" clearly has different connotations in Member countries.

In the UK, advisers are local education authority (i.e. employer) officers and therefore have a dual role: inspection and advice. A recent study of their innovative roles and training needs (Bolam et al. 1976) concludes that they spent a great deal of their time running short INSET courses and giving individual advice to teachers and that they wanted to carry on doing so. However, they are under some pressure from the community to emphasise their inspectorial and evaluative work which they were much less inclined to do.

In the USA the term is apparently used in a sense which is closely similar to Havelock's "consultant":

"The Advisory Approach to in-service is characterised by the non threatening, sustained and intimate relationship the adviser develops not only with the teacher but with the children as well."
(US 129)

The advisory or consultancy role is of great potential value in INSET and, where it exists, certainly requires closer study and documentation.

One of the principal new types of INSET institution to emerge recently is some form of teachers' or education centre. The UK report appraises the work of teachers'centres somewhat critically (UK Case 4) and presents three views of the professional centre concept (UK 106 and Cases 1 and 2). The rationale for Australian centres includes community participation (A 42) and several examples are described (A 44, 67, 79 and 84). According to the Dutch report, teachers' centres are not seen as having a major role in future INSET developments (N 76). In Germany INSET centres exist at several levels (GS German introduction); in Sweden there are the larger university-linked centres and municipality centres (S 19); in Japan (J 32) there are educational research and training centres; and in France there is a network of Pedagogical Documentation Research Centres (F 5) and sixteen Research Institutes for the Teaching of Mathematics (F 13). In America, teachers centres are said to be characterised by "greater teacher involvement autonomy and self-direction" (US 18) although their frequent collaboration with universities (US 125) distinguishes them from their English counterpart and raises numerous governance issues.

The actual and potential contributions at such centres certainly requires more detailed study. A typology of centres and the identification of critical dimensions would also be valuable. A start has been made in America where, for example, one seminar participant has distinguished between seven types of centre (Yarger, 1974):

1. the independent teacher centre;
2. the almost independent teacher centre;
3. the professional organisation teacher centre;
4. the single unit teacher centre;
5. the free partnership teacher centre;
6. the pre-consortium teacher centre;
7. the legislative-political consortium teacher centre.

Several innovative uses of traditional institutions are reported, one of which - INSET for teachers alongside experienced members of other professions - was raised in the seminar and mentioned in a British casestudy (UK 39). In Australia (A 14) certain professional associations are providing INSET. In Italy the OPPI is now exclusively for INSET (I 16). In Canada, the Atlantic Institute of Education is a consortium of agencies, including universities, which provides a flexible approach to INSET and 'focuses on the needs of those working in schools' (C 47).

Perhaps the most significant innovation in the new use of traditional agencies is the rapid and extensive growth of interest in school-focused or school-based INSET. In Sweden, study-days have a school-focused orientation and have been operating for some years; two uses of such study-days are reported (S Cases 2 and 3). In Australia the idea is taking root in a variety of forms (A Case 6). The UK report offers a tentative typology of school-based INSET based upon diverse experience and practice and also sounds several notes of caution (UK Case 5). In Japan, the school-based researchers are also INSET coordinators (J 46). The American report contains several references to job-embedded INSET, local staff development initiatives and the need to train school-based trainers (e.g. US 23, 77, 136).

At national level several innovative approaches to the utilisation of INSET agents are reported. For example in the UK 20 per cent of staff time in colleges of education is, in future, to be given over to INSET work but this policy is not proving easy to implement (UK 103). Another significant national strategy received only passing mention at the Philadelphia seminar and in the US reports, presumably because it is so widely prevalent and well established that it is no longer regarded as innovative.

The Teacher Corps was established in 1965, on the model of the Peace Corps, to enlist mainly young and inexperienced teachers for one year's work in city slums and areas of rural poverty. However, major changes have since occurred and its present approach is summarised in the following quotations from a presidential Advisory Committed (NACEPD, 1975):

"Substantial amendments to Teacher Corps occurred in 1974 under provisions of PL 93-380. The legislation authorized Teacher Corps to provide support for demonstration projects to retrain experienced educational personnel serving in local educational agencies. Under the previous law, the Teacher Corps could enroll experienced teachers only if they were leading teaching teams consisting of inexperienced teacher-interns."

"Under the guidelines prepared for the new Tenth Cycle Teacher Corps grants, projects may emphasize one of five areas:

- training complex, meaning variations on the teacher center idea;
- competency-based teacher education;
- training for implementing alternative school designs;
- interdisciplinary training approaches;
- training for the systematic adoption of research findings."

"The Teacher corps is trying to show that for change to occur in the schools, the entire school staff should be involved and be supportive of the changes being implemented."

"Teacher Corps operates on the basis of a system of project grants to an average of about fifty grantees in each Teacher Corps cycle. A "project" is jointly developed by an institution of higher education and a local education agency, a proposal is submitted to Teacher Corps-Washington, and a panel of reviewers determines which of these proposals will receive grants. Grantees are chosen on the basis of how well their proposals appear to meet the criteria set forth in the guidelines, and other considerations, as determined by the reviewers."

INSET agents and agencies operate at all system levels. They are numerous and their characteristics, their strengths and weaknesses and the tasks with which they are best-fitted to deal, vary considerably both within and between countries. As the principal INSET resource it is vital that they are thoroughly studied in a research and development context. National and international typologies which identify their significant distinguishing features are essential. So too is an indication of the external support structure necessary for their sustenance and improvement. For example, what kind of financial and collaborative governance procedures do the various agencies need and what kind of initial, induction and in-service education, training and support do the various agents need?

A key dimension in these typologies will undoubtedly be the change strategies and methods open to the INSET agent. The innovation process model assumes that INSET agents and agencies choose from several strategies and methods to achieve their objectives. A fundamental distinction can be made between power-coercive (or political-administrative), empirical-rational and normative-reeducative strategies (Bennis et al. 1969; Hoyle, 1970).

VI

INSET STRATEGIES AND METHODS

The relevance of the three change strategies - power-coercive, empirical-rational and normative-reeducative - is explored first in relation to the formulation of policy on the aims and structure of INSET. We first need to note that policy decision-makers at all levels, while retaining their authority and power to take decisions (the power-coercive strategy) nowadays frequently adopt the political-administrative varient of consulting extensively before making a decision.

1. TEACHER PARTICIPATION IN THE GOVERNANCE OF INSET

There is evidence of a trend towards increased teacher participation in INSET planning procedures. Consultative committees, representing the three main interest groups - employers, providing agencies and teachers - in roughly equal proportions, are being established at local authority level in England and Wales although by no means on a uniform basis (UK 6, 109). Teacher participation is guaranteed by regulation in Sweden (S 9) and is possibly most directly influential in the planning of study days (S 39). The Australian report refers to growing teacher involvement as a strength in current INSET developments (A 109). However, elsewhere the situation is more confused (e.g. F 6, J iii).

The question "who controls INSET?" is becoming of increasing importance and is leading to a concern for devising appropriate collaborative, governance machinery (e.g. Smith, 1975, UK 6). There are at least three main reasons underlying this trend. First, unlike pre-service teacher education, INSET does not normally have clearly defined institutional bases and organisational infrastructures. Second, INSET has been widely criticised as being too theoretical and insufficiently relevant to the practical needs of teachers and schools. Third, there is a powerful movement for teachers to participate in educational decision making in general and in decisions affecting INSET in particular. These three arguments are fairly widely prevalent but are particularly relevant to the growth and management of various forms of Teachers' Centre (e.g. Yarger, 1974, A 47).

Certain key issues in the governance of INSET appear to be common. Naturally the cultural and contextual factors vary from one country to another, but it does seem feasible to attempt to discuss these issues in terms of generalisable dimensions, and the innovation process model is reasonably helpful in this respect.

A. The Change Agent System

a) Level: governance issues arise at four main system levels in an education system: national; regional or state; local; and institutional (e.g. school).

b) INSET Agents: at least seven main INSET agents are distinguishable:

   i) national government
   ii) state/regional government
   iii) local government
   iv) providing agencies including schools
   v) teachers and their professional associations
   vi) community groups
   vii) "commercial groups" e.g. publishers, R and D agencies and TV/radio broadcasters.

c) Strategies: INSET governance organisations usually have access to two types of power or change strategy:

   i) Executive: i.e. the power to control policy through coercive or political-administrative means;
   ii) Consultative: i.e. the power to influence or advise on policy through empirical-rational (and occasionally normative re-educative) means.

B. Innovations or Tasks

The five main INSET tasks identified in Section IV were:

a) Release and financing of teachers to undertake INSET
b) Content and methods of INSET programmes and activities
c) Validation of INSET awards
d) Accreditation and certification related to INSET awards
e) Co-ordination of INSET provision.

C. Target User Systems

These will vary with the task but the seven interest groups identified as INSET agents (A.b. above) will usually be involved. When the INSET agent (e.g. a university) decides to adopt a consultative strategy then representatives from the target users (e.g. teachers) will be invited to participate in some form of consultative or collaborative process.

The validity and usefulness of this analytic framework can only be established by applying and modifying it in particular national contexts.

The following Section does this for the UK system, with which the writer is most familiar, at local level. A local area may be regarded as coterminous with but separate from the area controlled by the local education authority.

a) Release and finance for INSET

At present, if a UK teacher applies for a course requiring release, the head of his school and the LEA take the crucial decisions, i.e. they carry out an executive function. The national Induction and In-Service Training committee (INIST) has, however, recently recommended that consultative groups with substantial teacher representation should be established at both levels to advise the heads and LEAs about these tasks.

b) Programme Structure and Content

In the UK, INSET providing agencies have to formulate policies on such matters as which courses should be award-bearing, at what level (e.g. Ph.D., Masters, Bachelors, Diploma) these awards should be made, how long the course should be and whether it should be based on a modular or traditional basis. At present executive decisions about the structure and content of INSET programmes are taken internally by the appropriate staff of the main providing agencies i.e. universities, polytechnics, colleges of education and institutes of higher education. Some of these agencies have established consultative groups representing teachers and LEAs and INIST has recommended that this practice should be extended. In teachers' centres these executive decisions are taken by the warden and LEA inspectors but most centres have consultative committees. It is less clear how far LEA inspectors take "executive" decisions about the content and structure of their own courses without reference to anybody. Within any one school the "executive" function for internally provided INSET decisions rests formally with the head: INIST has recommended the setting up of consultative procedures with schools to cover this.

c) Validation of INSET Awards

Validation decisions about the standard of any particular award or course are usually taken by the academics of the institution concerned, often in consultation with external examiners from a similar institution. This is best exemplified in established universities which jealously guard their validation prerogatives for first and higher degrees and diplomas. The coming of the Council for National Academic Awards has led to increased teacher participation.

d) Accreditation and Certification

Certification is a national responsibility in the UK and to a large extent the credits (e.g. salary increment) attached to any particular course are also nationally negotiated. However, largely informal accreditation judgements are apparently made when teachers apply for promotion.

e) Co-ordination

A number of local areas have now established some form of machinery and the following features are worth noting: they have usually come about on the initiative of the LEA; an LEA administrator or inspector usually chairs the meetings; the LEA usually provides secretarial support; there is no common pattern of teacher and providing agency representation; it is not always clear whether they are designed to provide advice to the LEA in its providing agency role, to act as joint consultation machinery to co-ordinate INSET or to enable the LEA to co-ordinate provision in its area.

One alternative would be to specify the committee's task as co-ordination and its function as exclusively advisory/consultative (i.e. it would have no executive power). The chairmanship and provision of secretarial support would then be a joint or consecutive responsibility of providers, LEA and teachers. At present there is no significant demand for community representation, though "commercial" interests are represented to varying extents.

Table 6.1 highlights some of these issues at local level and similar issues are relevant at national and regional levels. The analytic framework is obviously crude and is therefore offered for modification and adaptation. Certain tasks (e.g. the collection of research data) have been ignored because they do not bear upon the central issues.

2. TRAINING METHODS

Within the three principal strategies mentioned above, the INSET agent has access to numerous and various modes and methods of communicating the content of any specific programme. Adapting Havelock, 1969, we may distinguish between six modes of knowledge dissemination:

a) social-interaction - a largely unplanned and informal, centre-periphery mode;

b) research, development and diffusion - a planned and formal, centre-periphery mode;

Table 6.1. INSET GOVERNANCE MACHINERY AT LOCAL LEVEL:
TASKS, STRUCTURES AND POWERS

TASK 1: RELEASE AND FINANCING

| L.E.A. EMPLOYER || SCHOOL ||
EXECUTIVE	CONSULTATIVE	EXECUTIVE	CONSULTATIVE
Local Inspectorate	Representative Committee?	Head/ Principal	Staff Committee (including professional tutor or equivalent)?

TASK 2: STRUCTURE AND CONTENT

| UNIVERSITY/COLLEGE/POLY INST. H.E./TEACHERS' CENTRE || L.E.A. EMPLOYER || SCHOOL ||
EXECUTIVE	CONSULTATIVE	EXECUTIVE	CONSULTATIVE	EXECUTIVE	CONSULTATIVE
Internal Staff	Representative Committee?	Local Inspectorate	?	Head/ Principal	Staff Committee (including professional tutor or equivalent)?

TASK 3: VALIDATION OF AWARDS

| UNIVERSITY/COLLEGE/POLY INST. H.E./TEACHERS' CENTRE ||
EXECUTIVE	CONSULTATIVE
Internal Staff and External Examiners	Representative Committee?

TASK 4: ACCREDITATION AND CERTIFICATION

| L.E.A. EMPLOYER ||
EXECUTIVE	CONSULTATIVE
Local Inspectorate	?

TASK 5: COORDINATION OF PROVISION

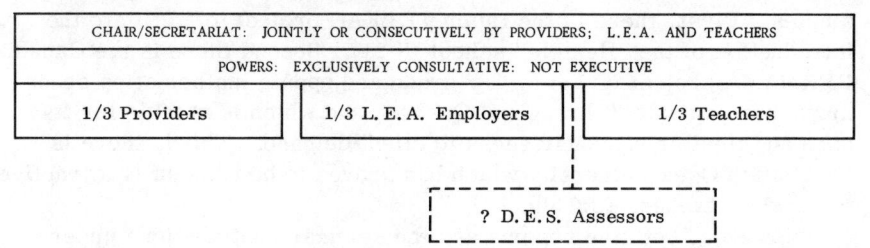

| CHAIR/SECRETARIAT: JOINTLY OR CONSECUTIVELY BY PROVIDERS; L.E.A. AND TEACHERS |||
POWERS: EXCLUSIVELY CONSULTATIVE: NOT EXECUTIVE		
1/3 Providers	1/3 L.E.A. Employers	1/3 Teachers

? D.E.S. Assessors

37

c) problem-solving user - stresses the perspective of the user as a rational and systematic problem-solver, seeking and using externally provided information and help;

d) task-consultancy - aims to help users with their tasks and problems (e.g. curriculum development);

e) process-consultancy - aims to help users with the underlying processes (e.g. decision-making procedures) and is central to the normative-re-educative strategy;

f) linkage - Havelock argues the need for a new agency to provide linkage and articulation for the agencies involved in modes a to e.

Within the three fundamental strategies and the six modes, the INSET agent is also able to choose from a variety of methods for communication (e.g. print or t.v.), training (e.g. lecture or workshop), evaluation design (e.g. classical or illuminative) and dissemination (e.g. learned journal or tape-slide presentation). The strategy, mode and methods chosen will vary with the nature of each INSET task or programme and with the relationship between the INSET agent and the user system.

These theoretical considerations help to set some aspects of the national reports in perspective. Several reports criticise INSET for being insufficiently practical and some criticise centre-periphery or top-down strategies of curriculum development and innovation as being ineffective. One solution offered by the Australian (A 84, 92), UK (97, 110) and German/Swiss (GS 68, 80) reports is to regard the school as a problem solving or creative system which requires external support, particularly INSET of various kinds and from various agencies. The various types of teachers' centres appear to be fulfilling a linkage role and the advisory approach mentioned in Section IV is in the process-consultancy tradition. Both in the Australian report and in his seminar contribution, Skilbeck stressed the importance of curriculum development as the key task area in which teachers would welcome task consultancy (c.f. Skilbeck, 1976).

Major developments have taken place in the application of distance teaching methods to INSET. The case studies include three good examples. First, there is the Dutch TELEAC project to facilitate the introduction of the "flexible" school (N 21). Second there is the Canadian PERMAMA project (C 16) to "up-grade and update mathematics secondary school teachers" throughout Quebec, and which is notable for its open and flexible responsibeness to client demand. Third, there is the British Open University which has proved to be especially attractive to serving teachers (UK 50).

However, both the reports and the seminar contributions understandably gave greater prominence to INSET agencies and strategies than to methods. Yet there clearly is need for a typology of methods and a critical assessment of their relative strengths and weaknesses. Havelock's 1969 framework makes some useful general distinctions, for example between one and two way transmissions and between dyadic, small group and large group exchange. What is needed now is to build upon and modify this general framework in terms of its specific application to INSET.

The typology would thus include methods of general applicability in other fields (e.g. lectures, programmed learning, distance teaching and group discussion) but would also include methods of much more specific relevance. The following are examples of these:

a) <u>Consultancy</u>: at least two approaches have been used successfully with school faculties: organisation development (Schmuck and Miles, 1971) and an approach in the Tavistock Institute tradition (Richardson, 1973). Analogous approaches with individuals include counselling and micro-counselling (Ivey and Rollin, 1974) and clinical supervision (Cogan, 1973).

b) <u>Problem Solving User</u>: relevant methods here include various forms of staff development (Pratt, 1973); allocated days for staff conferences (S 82; UK 87); demonstration teaching, including team teaching where this is one of its aims (e.g. Waterhouse, 1976) and resources centres (Holder and Newton, 1973).

c) <u>Analytic Skills</u>: the methods which we may loosely and tentatively include in this category are various self-rating scales of a traditional kind (e.g. the Stanford Teacher Competence Appraisal Guide) and innovative kind, for example the self-monitoring techniques devised for the Ford T. project (Elliot and Adelman, 1973). Similarly there are classroom analysis techniques of a more established kind (e.g. Flanders, 1970) and of an innovative kind, for example rooted in phenomenological theory (e.g. Delamont, 1976). Tools for analysing curriculum innovations have been devised by Eraut et al. 1975 and by Hull and Wells, undated. Tools for institutional self-analysis have been devised by the IMTEC project (Dalin, 1975) and by the Centre for New Schools (Moore, 1972).

d) <u>Simulations</u>: a wide variety of simulation materials and methods now exist. These include critical incidents, case studies and in-baskets (e.g. Perry and Perry, 1969 and Taylor, 1973), micro-teaching (Allen and Ryan, 1969) and less well-known methods like the case-conference technique (Clarke and Pococke, 1971). Protocol materials undoubtedly represent the most sophisticated approach to simulation though at least one practitioner thinks they have over-emphasised protocols related to concepts at the expense of those related to teaching skills (Cruikshank, 1974).

e) <u>Competency- Based Methods</u>: this major development in American pre-service teacher training is now making an impact on INSET (US 136) and indeed on the training of administrators (Lipham, 1975). Competency-based approaches to teacher training had two quite different stimuli: community pressures for accountability and the desire to be more specific about training objectives. The extension of CBTE to INSET carried with it all the dangers and strengths of this dual ancestry. A balanced and not uncritical account of CBTE was prepared by a presidential advisory committee (NACEPD, 1976). Because of its comprehensive and radical nature it could prove to be one of the most significant innovations in this field and its influence is beginning to be felt outside the US (Evans, 1976).

f) <u>INSET Training Package</u>: numerous training packages have now been produced. These vary widely in terms of aims and structure. They aim at staff development (Jung, 1972), at training for change (Havelock and Havelock, 1973), at particular pedagogical skills like reading (UK 54, 58) and at particular subjects like Science (A Case 2).

This selection is not intended to be comprehensive: the examples necessarily reflect the writer's interests. However, the wide variety and number of INSET methods is clearly demonstrated and the need for an analytic and critical typology is surely equally clear, not least because of its implications and potential value for the training of trainers.

3. RESEARCH AND EVALUATION

The dominant impression gained from the reports is that much less has been achieved in this area than in the others. Dr. John Hopkins was the introductory speaker for this theme and although he began by confirming this impression he also stressed that teacher INSET was far from unique in not having developed satisfactory evaluation tools. He linked this gap to the lack of agreement and clarity about INSET aims and objectives which was discussed under theme 1 and went on to outline some of the underlying and general conceptual and practical difficulties facing the evaluators of action programmes.

The most frequently reported form of evaluation in the case studies involved asking the target group or participants to rate the course or programme of activities, thus providing a summative appraisal. The Open University's techniques are both formative and summative, although they use written course and examination papers as the principal evidence of achievement. Neither of these approaches to evaluation attempt to cover the effects of INSET on teaching performance and no such attempt is reported, although the American report hints at it (e.g. US 96 and 136).

This reflects the fundamental dilemma confronting the would-be evaluator of INSET: how to devise valid and reliable instruments for activities which are generally not amenable to an evaluation based upon output measures. Experience from curriculum evaluation indicates that, while these difficulties should be tackled, they should not prevent attempts to make progress on other fronts and the reports indicate that this lesson has been learned, particularly with respect to the evaluation of the ongoing process of INSET. One of the Netherlands case studies (N 61) describes the systematic, formative evaluation discussions between participants and lecturers on the creative arts project. Both the Canadian studies stress open, ongoing evaluation as an important feature of the innovations. The teacher induction schemes are being evaluated in a similar concurrent fashion (UK 23).

Procedures for costing INSET activities vary considerably from country to country and the information on costing in the reports is scanty and scattered. Without similar data bases, which may be dependent on some agreed typology of INSET, it is unclear what meaningful comparative costing statements can be made.

Sweden has probably introduced the most comprehensibe and systematic approaches to evaluation (S Cases 4 and 2), many of them designed to inform decision-makers, and this orientation is also being adopted in Australia (A 69). Several studies argue the need for an adequate research data-base for the national INSET system as a whole (N 20, A 33, UK 113). American efforts in this direction appear to be comprehensive (US 139) but, nevertheless, even there a powerful plea is made for more extensive work (US 51).

In the light of the reports and the seminar, we may differentiate between at least five different activities on which evaluation might focus:

a) The first is the external and possibly large-scale evaluation carried out by researchers. Methodological and research design issues are particularly relevant here.

b) A national and regional/state level, there appears to be an urgent need for an improvement in the INSET data base. At present there is a serious lack of information and research about vitally important aspects of INSET, though the Swedish approach is instructive. One first step would be to identify appropriate strategies and procedures for the regular collection of the following sorts of survey data:

teacher needs; system needs; available resources; ongoing activities and programmes; evaluation procedures; costs; research and development activities; consultation and planning procedures.

c) Providing agencies also appear to have an urgent need for simple and straightforward evaluation methods which can be used by practitioners for two purposes: formative and summative course evaluation; self-monitoring of the providing agency's overall INSET programme.

d) A great deal of attention was paid in both the national reports and the Philadelphia conference itself to school-based or school-focused INSET. Moreover, as indicated above, one of the main follow-up activities will deal with this area. Here, too, there is a need for simple and straightforward procedures and strategies to enable schools to plan and monitor their staff development and INSET activities.

e) Individual trainers need simple and straightforward summative and self-monitoring procedures for their clinical counselling and supervisory interactions with individual teachers.

More fundamentally there is considerable need for clarification of relevant research and evaluation concepts. Table 6.2 applies the innovation process model to the two main INSET task areas, as elaborated in Section V. In so doing, the corresponding research and evaluation task areas are identified and a series of important questions are generated.

Table 6.2. INSET RESEARCH AND EVALUATION (R + E)

1. FOCUS OF R + E	2. R + E AGENT	3. USER OF R + E	4. R + E STRATEGY + METHODS
Policy and Structure National Regional/State Local Institutional	Internal or External?	Internal or External?	"Agricultural- Botany" or "Illuminative"?
Providing Agency Policy and Programmes External Internal Individual	Internal or External?	Internal or External?	"Agricultural- Botany" or "Illuminative"?

Column 1 identifies the two main task areas for research and evaluation. The first is overall INSET policy and structure at national, regional/state, local and institutional levels. The second is policy and programmes in the following types of providing agency: external (e.g. colleges and teachers' centres), internal (e.g. the school itself) and the individual (e.g. the teacher).

Column 2 asks whether the evaluator is the system itself (i.e. self-monitoring) or an outsider. The relationship between evaluator and "client" is of great importance: for example, evaluation by employers and by independent, funded evaluators pose very different problems and issues in, say, the initial negotiation of entry for the evaluator (cf. Stake, 1976).

Column 3 asks a fundamental question: who is the evaluation for? Will the funding body control use and access of the data? Or will the subjects of the evaluation have joint control (cf. MacDonald, 1976)?

Column 4 asks questions about the evaluation strategy and methods to be adopted. In the last fifteen years, professional opinion has shifted considerably from the position classically expounded by Campbell and Stanley, 1963. Research designs in the "illuminative" tradition are now widely used whereas, in the past, only those in the "agricultural-botany" tradition were acceptable (Parlett and Hamilton, 1972). This, in turn, has led to the use of newer "instruments" like the case study and "portrayal" (Stake, 1976).

INSET evaluation is in its very early stages and it therefore needs to take account of work in related fields, viz.:

a) evaluation research (e.g. Weiss, 1972; Guba, 1975),

b) organisation development (e.g. Schmuck et al. 1971),

c) survey feedback (e.g. Schmuck and Miles, 1971),

d) industrial management training (e.g. Warr et al. 1970),

e) innovation studies (e.g. McLaughlin, 1976; Havelock and Havelock, 1973),

f) clinical supervision (e.g. Cogan, 1973).

However, unlike the situation in the pedagogy of INSET, the basic typologies of educational evaluation do exist (e.g. Campbell and Stanley, 1963; Stake, 1976; Jenkins, 1976). The task is to specify their various dimensions more clearly and to apply them and the overall typologies to INSET. A necessary first step, however, will be to review INSET evaluation practices on a national basis.

4. DISSEMINATION AND GENERALISABILITY

In introducing this aspect of theme 4, Dr. John Hopkins maintained that the existing state of INSET knowledge did not allow for the generalisation of validated approaches. Certainly, the task of adapting or generalising INSET concepts, procedures, programmes and materials raises major practical problems which tended to be left implicit in most of the reports. The Australian study does provide one instructive example of the adaptation of a science programme (A Case 2) and similar materials development exercises probably offer the best means of sharing practical experience. The interest in induction and internship does suggest that other tasks can also be the subject of meaningful international exchange, provided that the fundamental contextual variants are recognised. However, there was general endorsement of Dr. Hopkins' view that some priority be given to an overall research and development strategy which would, amongst other things, make clearer what kind of INSET approaches were generalisable. This view found further support from a brief seminar account of a National Council, funded by Teacher Corps, to facilitate inter-state communication about INSET (National Council of States on In-Service Education, 1976). Several seminar participants urged the adoption of this approach both in individual countries and, on an international basis, by OECD for Member countries.

The innovation process model can be applied to this task as it was to evaluation and Havelock's, 1969, typology of knowledge diffusion processes ought to provide a useful framework for classifying analogous work in INSET. There are certainly enough examples which would repay study: the adaptation of micro-teaching materials (CERI, 1975); the adaptation of CBTE materials (Liverpool Teachers' Centre, 1976); the take-up of Open University materials and methods in other countries; the Colleges of Education CELPP project strategy (NCET, 1972); the adaptation of the STEP materials (A Case 2); the use of the R - D and D. approach in the American Regional laboratories (e.g. Jung, 1972); the Protocol Materials strategy (Burdin, 1974); the American Training the Teacher Trainers strategy; and the Teacher Corps strategy.

It seems clear that training strategies are most easily packaged for dissemination since they are less culture and context bound than are agency structures and particular programme contents. However, the fate of analogous curriculum training packages for pupils and students in the compulsory schooling period is not always encouraging. A great deal can be learned from that experience (e.g. Fullan and Pomfret, 1975) and particular attention will need to be paid to the needs of the users of such training packages.

VII

SOME INTERIM CONCLUSIONS

This report set out to achieve four main aims: to summarise and synthesise the interim outcomes of the first phase of the project; to identify the main policy issues; to explore the utility of a provisional conceptual framework; and to identify needed research and development activities to which CERI might contribute.

The difficulties of summarising and synthesising the outcomes of ten contextual reports, thirty-five case studies and a one-week international seminar are obvious enough. The sheer range and quality of the many on-going INSET approaches portrayed in the reports and seminar contributions is much less to be expected. In several countries, INSET appears to have reached a take-off position. The post-1973 economic recession has undoubtedly had severe effects but one's strong impression is that the take-off has been postponed, not cancelled.

Perhaps the most striking feature of both the reports and the seminar was the apparent agreement amongst professional associations, teacher educators and governments in Member countries about two conclusions: first, the overall importance of INSET and, second, the need to give it high priority within national education policies. Why should this be so?

The justification offered for allocating scarce resources to INSET was that it would improve the quality of education in schools. Thus, the main aims of INSET were generally agreed to be the improvement of teachers' performance in their classrooms and schools and professional development in the wider sense of encouraging individual teachers to monitor and shape their own careers.

The drastically reduced demand for teachers was regarded as the main argument for giving high priority to INSET at this particular point in time. The effect of this reduced demand, together with the high level of general unemployment, has been to stabilise the teaching force both within schools and within local education authorities and school systems. This pronounced trend is currently being most felt in primary schools, but secondary schools, too, are experiencing it and will do so even more in the next few years. The advantages of a stable teaching force are apparent, particularly following a period of high teacher mobility and turnover: students and schools should certainly benefit in the short term. However, most participants were agreed that stability could too easily lead to stagnation in the longer term. The external pressures and demands upon schools are likely to alter rather than to moderate. If teachers are to be in a position to respond professionally and constructively to legitimate pressures to change and also to distinguish these from those which are merely meretricious, then they need continuing INSET. Many participants were also convinced that for these reasons INSET should be given priority over pre-service education and training (PRESET) if necessary.

There was also agreement about the nature of some of the major contextual factors to which INSET ought to be directed. Those that were particularly mentioned in the seminar include the curricular problems associated with the extension of the compulsory schooling age to sixteen, and particularly the needs of the 13-16 age group; the needs of immigrant groups and multi-ethnic communities; needs associated with particular subjects, notably science and mathematics; the new demands on teachers caused by the radically changing nature of school-community relationships, for instance in new arrangements for school governance; the curricular and organisational consequence of falling student numbers, especially in secondary schools; the strategic need to ensure effective internal school management through the training of principals and senior teachers at middle management levels.

The priority given to these and similar major tasks will naturally vary but their vital importance was widely acknowledged as, too, were their implications for INSET. There was less agreement about some of the questions they raise concerning the relative merits of compulsory and voluntary INSET. These issues can be posed in terms of incentives for teachers to engage in INSET. Experience in some countries indicates that for many teachers, especially those in primary schools, the intrinsic motivation of improving one's capacity to educate children is sufficient incentive for some purposes. On the other hand, countries have also found it necessary to introduce compulsory INSET for particular purposes. The possibilities between these two approaches include strengthening the relevance of INSET by, for example, school-focused methods and by offering short rather than long courses; giving teachers an entitlement to adequate release time to enable them to attend INSET in school time; offering various credits and awards at the conclusion of INSET courses; these may or may not be carefully articulated one with another and may or may not lead to an automatic salary increase. While it was recognised that these were profoundly important issues, there was no general agreement, even within Member countries, about the desirability and effectiveness of these approaches.

There did appear to be general agreement that the needs of the individual professional teacher should receive due attention. The actual and potential contribution of various forms of teachers' centre to this end was clear. So, too, was the role of the college of education either on its own or in some kind of collaborative arrangement with other agencies. The availability of experienced staff and valuable college resources freed by the reductions in initial teacher training were a powerful economic and logistic reason for strengthening INSET.

It often proved difficult to identify precise areas of agreement and disagreement because of the inherent problems of defining and conceptualising INSET rather than because of the normal problems of understanding differing cultural and political contexts. It is for this reason that an attempt has been made in this report, perhaps, prematurely, to formulate a conceptual framework for continuing professional development in education, including INSET. The innovation process model (see Appendix 3) adopts the perspective of the change agent within an open-systems framework. Hence, it pays particular attention to the characteristics of contextual factors, the user, policies and programmes, agents and agencies and their strategies and methods for governance and decision-making, training, evaluation and dissemination. These factors are all considered at five levels: national, regional/state, local, institutional and individual.

No doubt this model has some serious weaknesses and gaps. The allocation of concepts and issues to a particular section was frequently rather arbitrary. The dubiousness of the implication that innovations and INSET tasks are conceptually synonymous was very evident in the discussion of INSET policy and structure: a more direct use of systems theory (Davies, 1975) might well be more satisfactory. However, this in turn would add weight to the charge that the framework is far too eclectic, although it is surely difficult to avoid eclecticism in a field which embraces as many activities and disciplines as INSET. Notwithstanding these and other possible criticisms, the provisional framework is offered for discussion, assessment, modification and, indeed, rejection as the conceptualisation of INSET moves out of its present early stage of development.

The framework has been used as the basis for organising some of the key policy issues which appear to emerge from this first phase of the project. In accordance with the spirit of Rubin's argument (US 51), no particular ordering of priorities is implied by the sequence of questions and issues which follows. The answers will, of course, differ from one country to another.

1. Contextual Issues at National, Regional/State, Local and Institutional Levels:

    i) What kind of legal framework is necessary and feasible for INSET?
    ii) How much release and funding for INSET should a teacher be entitled to in, say, a forty-year career?
    iii) Should INSET be given priority over pre-service education and training?
    iv) Should funds be specifically earmarked for INSET?
    v) What are the implications of the accountability movement for INSET?

vi) How can political support and funding be obtained for release-based INSET when teachers receive much longer vacations than the average worker?

vii) What are a teacher's professional obligations in relation to INSET?

2. INSET Users

i) Is there an appropriate conceptual framework for INSET?

ii) Do adequate procedures exist for establishing the needs of INSET users?

iii) In what ways are non-teacher education professionals regarded as INSET users?

iv) What specific contributions can INSET make to the professionalisation of educators?

v) In what way are the community and parents seen as INSET users?

vi) How helpful is the "career profile" notion as a guide to identifying INSET needs?

vii) What priority should be given to induction INSET programmes for beginning teachers? Are they regarded as strategically important in opening up the INSET system?

viii) What is the comparative importance, as incentives to engage in INSET, of salary increments, promotion, university credits and release time?

ix) Are teachers sufficiently regarded as adult learners by INSET trainers?

x) To what extent is INSET regarded as part of a wider structure of continuing or recurrent education?

3. Tasks: Policies and Programmes

i) Is there an adequate policy and programme design framework?

ii) What are the principal components of the task of INSET policy formulation and implementation at national, regional/state, local and institutional levels?

iii) To what extent are INSET programmes devised along lines similar to those in the curriculum process model?

iv) Is there an undue emphasis on programmes designed to meet systems rather than individual needs?

v) What kind of programmes meet the needs of individual professionals?

vi) What priority should be given to programmes for particular target groups e.g. principals, beginning teachers, inner city teachers?

vii) Is curriculum development-linked INSET the best way to ensure relevance?

viii) What are the main implications of INSET linked to other professions for the content of teacher INSET?

4. Resources: Agents and Agencies

   i) Is there an adequate support framework for INSET?
   ii) To what extent have the various resources been identified and rationalised according to cost benefit criteria?
   iii) What contribution do professional associations make as providing agencies?
   iv) What are the comparative strengths and weaknesses of teachers, college lecturers, inspectors and advisers as INSET agents?
   v) What part can and do school-based staff play in INSET and research and development?
   vi) To what extent have the training needs of the various INSET agents been systematically studied and met?
   vii) Do teachers have adequate access to books, libraries and other resources for their individual INSET activities?
   viii) What are the key distinguishing features of each type of INSET agency (e.g. teachers' centre, college)?
   ix) What are the principal components of successful school-focused or job-embedded programmes?

5. Strategies and Methods

   i) Is there adequate decision-making machinery for formulating INSET policies and programmes at all five levels of the system?
   ii) To what extent do teachers participate at each system level in decisions concerning release and finance, programme content and methods, validation of awards, accreditation and certification, and the coordination of INSET provision?
   iii) Is there an adequate pedagogical framework for INSET training methods?
   iv) What research and development work is on-going to assess the utility of the numerous training methods now available?
   v) Is there an adequate research and evaluation framework for INSET at each system level?
   vi) What research and development work is on-going to assess the utility of the numerous evaluation methods now available?
   vii) Is there an adequate dissemination framework for INSET at each system level?
   viii) What research and development work is on-going to assess the utility of the various dissemination strategies now available?

The Philadelphia seminar ended on a note of enthusiastic commitment to the pursuance of future international activities and several possibilities were considered. One concerned the actual and potential role of distance teaching methods in INSET. Another concerned ways of improving the induction or internship period because this was inherently desirable and because of light it might throw upon problems of linkage and coordination between the initial and in-service stages of teacher education and training. A third, which concerned the need to explore ways of strengthening and extending the existing international network for the dissemination of information on INSET, might be worth immediate consideration, particularly with respect to the important role that CERI might play in such a network.

In the light of the national reports and the seminar discussions, one of the aims of this interim synthesis report has been to identify task areas which could form the basis for future work by CERI. The main criterion used was that the task area should be one in which the findings of international study could be generalisable or adaptable to particular national contexts. Six separate follow-up activities are outlined below. It is, of course, recognised that INSET is a "seamless robe". Nevertheless, these six activities can be usefully distinguished for analytic and practical purposes provided that their mutual implications are taken into account.

a) The Contribution of Adult Learning Theories and Practices to INSET

The seminar identified a strong need for research into adult learning theories as they apply to teachers. The vast experience of providing learning opportunities for adults outside the formal system of education and training has not yet penetrated the teacher training and retraining world. The following could be tackled:

1. The adaptation of the general knowledge base in adult learning to the specific needs of INSET programmes for teachers.
2. The relationships between continuing education, personal development, incentives of various kinds and career developments.
3. The specific implications of the predominance of women in the teaching profession.
4. The implications and possibilities of organising INSET for teachers alongside other "helping" professionals.

b) The Role of the School in INSET

There was virtual unanimity in the reports and at the seminar that the actual and potential role of the school in INSET ought to be explored and documented. This would call for a careful analysis of the conditions needed for the successful implementation of an approach which tries to respond to both teacher and the system needs. The following topics could be covered:

1. The definition of and rationale for school-focused training in the continuing training of teachers. What characterises schools which successfully operate such approaches?
2. The role of the "peer-group" and the emergence of new training roles: professional tutors, pedagogical advisers, research coordinators, consultants, etc.; the specific roles and training needs of those who facilitate school-focused INSET.
3. The characteristics and coordination of support structures for effective school-focused training, e.g. universities, colleges of education, research laboratories. Because of rapidly developing interest in and experience of them, the role of teachers' centres in school-focused INSET would repay particular study.
4. How can the effectiveness of school-focused INSET be evaluated? Is it cheaper than traditional approaches How can it be incorporated in an award-bearing structure (e.g. M. Eds. and Ph. Ds.)?

c) The Evaluation of INSET

There was general agreement among researchers, administrators and teacher educators about the urgent need for viable models and strategies for the evaluation of INSET. These needs should be studied at several levels:

1. A critical review of the theory and practice of evaluation in INSET and related fields like curriculum and action research.
2. The development of a comprehensive methodology for large scale and external evaluation of INSET programmes.
3. The development of methodologies for formative and summative evaluation of courses and programmes which can be easily administered internally by INSET providing agencies.
4. The improvement of the research and information base at regional and national levels so that the planning and implementation of INSET policies can be made more effective.
5. A consideration of the relationship of evaluation to the problems of identifying agreed aims for INSET at the five main system levels.

d) New INSET Materiels

INSET providing agencies and individuals have a central part to play in the improvement and development of effective INSET programmes, methods and materials.

1. What kinds of new INSET materials and approaches exist in Member countries, how effective are they and to what extent can they be adapted for use elsewhere?

2. What types of teacher training programmes can be developed that use, among other things, original and/or adapted training materials, self-directed and self-selected training experiences, distance teaching methods, performance-based methods, and applications of research findings to teaching? What problems must be resolved to make such a training programme functional?
3. Is one type of programme more effective than another in changing teachers? Changing pupils? Changing the organisational structure of the school?

e) Role and Training of Teacher Trainers

It therefore becomes of critical importance that trainers are adequately equipped in terms of skills and materials to carry out their task. A great deal of relevant work is currently on-going in Member countries and there is a need to identify those approaches which are adaptable and generalisable as a coherent sub-system of the teacher training system.

The major themes for future study include:

1. A survey of existing knowledge about the training needs of, and current training programmes for, the principal teacher trainers; this would be conducted in relation with the findings under a, b, c, and d above.
2. What are the merits of comprehensive national strategies for training teacher trainers compared with ad hoc approaches aimed at new roles (e.g. school-based professional tutors)?

f) INSET Finances and Resources

The reports revealed the paucity of comparable information which is currently available about existing INSET resources and costs. There is a clear need for a comparative study of at least three main espects of this problem.

1. Methods and procedures for utilising and providing for INSET at national, regional, local, institutional and programme levels.
2. Methods and procedures for calculating the costs of INSET at these same five levels.
3. Methods, procedures and problems of making international comparisons of INSET resources and costs at these five levels.

The ways in which CERI might tackle these six areas will no doubt vary from theme to theme. In cooperation with key consultants from Member countries, it could produce a series of monographs as the main output of this programme. The diagnoses suggested in such monographs, linked up with the already existing case-studies and the on-going follow-up activities which have already commenced in some Member countries, could thus make a practical and positive contribution to on-going discussions about INSET policies in OECD Member countries.

Appendix 1

BIBLIOGRAPHY

Part A. THE NATIONAL REPORTS

The following national reports, each containing detailed bibliographies, were published in 1976 by the Centre for Educational Research and Innovation, OECD, Paris, under the general title:

<u>Innovation in In-Service Education and Training of Teachers</u>

1.	Australia	M. Skilbeck, G. Evans and J. Harvey.
2.	Canada	M. Bélanger.
3.	France	G. Belbenoit.
4.	Germany/Switzerland	K. Frey, P. Posch, U. Kröll, J. Cavadini, U.P. Lattman, H. Fischler and K. Arregger.
5.	Italy	M. Reguzzoni.
6.	Japan	H. Azuma
7.	Netherlands	N. Deen and E.S. Boeder-Rijdes
8.	Sweden	S. Marklund and H. Eklund
9.	United Kingdom (not including Scotland and Northern Ireland)	R. Bolam and J. Porter
10.	United States of America	L. Rubin and K. Howey

Part B. SELECTIVE BIBLIOGRAPHY

This selective bibliography consists mainly of British and American studies because of the writer's familiarity with these sources. It is, of course, recognised that comparable work exists in other Member countries.

Allen, D.W. and Ryan, K., 1969, Micro-Teaching. New York: Addison-Wesley.

Bennis, W.G., Benne, K.D., and Chin, R., 1969, The Planning of Change. 2nd Edition, New York. Holt, Rinehart and Winston.

Bolam, R., 1973, Induction Programmes for Probationary Teachers. Bristol: The University of Bristol School of Education.

Bolam, R., 1974, Planned Educational Change: Theory and Practice. Bristol: University of Bristol School of Education.

Bolam, R., 1976, "The types of environment most likely to favour the active and effective participation of teachers in educational innovation"; New Patterns of Teacher Education and Tasks: Teachers as Innovators. Paris: OECD.

Bolam, R., Smith, G. and Canter, H., 1976, The LEA Adviser and Educational Innovation. Bristol: University of Bristol School of Education.

Bottoms, G., 1975, "Responsibilities of local school systems, state departments of education, institutions of higher education and professional organisations for in-service education". In Edelfelt, R.A. and Johnson, M. (eds.), 1975, Rethinking In-Service Education. Washington D.C.: National Education Association.

Burdin, J.L. 1974, "Questions on getting protocol materials into users' hands: marketing considerations". Journal of Teacher Education, 25.4.338.

Centre for Educational Research and Innovation, CERI, 1975, The International Transfer fo Micro-Teaching Programmes for Teacher Education. Paris: OECD.

Clark, J.M. and Pococke, S.E., 1971, "Teachers' role support during the probationary year", University of London, Institute of Education Bulletin, 24, Summer. Pp. 36-40.

Cruikshank, D.R., 1974, "The protocol materials movement: an examplar of efforts to wed theory and practice in teacher education". Journal of Teacher Education, 25.4.300-311.

Dalin, P., 1975, "International management training for educational change" in Hughes, M. (ed.) Administering Change: International Challenge. London: The Athlone Press of the University of London.

Davies, J., 1975, "A discussion of the use of PPBS and MBO in educational planning and administration". In Dobson, L., Gear T. and Westoby, A., Management in Education: Some Techniques and Systems. London: Ward Lock Educational.

Delamont, S., 1976, Interaction in the Classroom. London: Methuen.

Elliott, J. and Adelman, C., 1973, "Reflecting where the action is: the design of the Ford Teaching Project". Education for Teaching, 92. 8-20.

Eraut, M., Good, L. and Smith, G., 1975, The Analysis of Curriculum Materials. Brighton: University of Sussex.

Evans, L. E. M., 1976, The Teaching of Teaching. Duplicated conference report available from the Welsh Education Office, 16 Worcester Place, Swansea SA1 1JQ.

Ferry, G., 1974, "Experiments in continuing teacher training - France" in New Patterns of Teacher Education and Tasks. Paris OCDE.

Flanders, N.A., 1970, Analysing Teaching Behaviour. New York: Addison-Wesley.

Fullan, M. and Pomfret, A., 1975, Review of Research on Curriculum Implementation. Toronto: The Ontario Institute for Studies in Education, Department of Sociology.

Gross, N., Giacquinta, J.B. and Bernstein, M., 1971, Implementing Organisational Innovations. London: Harper and Row.

Guba, E., 1975, A Taxonomy of Problems Confronting the Practitioner of Educational Evaluation. Indiana University: Centre for the Study of Innovation.

Havelock, R.G., 1969, Planning for Innovation Through Dissemination and Utilization of Knowledge, Ann Arbor, Michigan: Centre for Research on Utilization of Scientific Knowledge.

Havelock, R.G. and Havelock, M.C., 1973, Training for Change Agents. Ann Arbor, Michigan: The University of Michigan, Institute for Social Research.

Holder, M. and Newton, E., 1973, "A school resource centre". British Journal of Educational Technology, 4.1.

Hoyle, E., 1970, "Planned organisational change in education", Research in Education, 3.

Hull, W. L. and Wells, R. L., undated, Innovations' Evaluation Guide. Columbus, Ohio: The Center for Vocational and Technical Education, The Ohio State University.

Jenkins, D., 1976, Six Alternative Models of Curriculum Evaluation. Unit 20 of Open University Course E203. Bletchley: Open University Press.

Joyce, B. R., 1976, A Study of In-Service Teacher Education: Concepts, User Needs and Literature. Palo Alto, California: Stanford Centre for Research and Development in Teaching.

Jung, C., 1972, "Institutional system for professional development". Theory into Practice, 11.5.276-284.

Lipham, J. M., 1975, "Competency/performance-based administrator education (C/P.B.A.E.): recent developments in the United States". In Hughes, M.G. (ed.) Administering Education: International Challenge London: The Athlone Press.

Liverpool Teachers' Centre, 1976, Teaching Supervision Training Programme. Liverpool: Gilmour Teachers' Centre.

Lomax, D., 1973, "Teacher education". In Butcher, J.J. and Pont, H.B. (eds.) Educational Research in Britain. London: University of London Press.

MacDonald, B., 1976, "Political classification of evaluation activity". In Tawney, D. (ed.), Curriculum Evaluation Today: Trends and Implications. Schools' Council Research Studies, London: Macmillan Educational.

McLaughlin, M.W., 1976, "Implementation as mutual adaptation: change in classroom organisation". In Teachers College Record, 77.3.339-351.

Moore, D., 1972, "Strengthening alternative high schools". Harvard Educational Review. Fall.

National Advisory Council on Education Professions Development, 1975, Teacher Corps: Past or Prologue? Washington D.C.: NACEPD.

National Advisory Council on Education Professions Development, 1976, Competency Based Teacher Education: Toward a Consensus. Washington D.C.: NACEPD.

(National) Council for Educational Technology, 1972, Educational Technology in Teacher Education and Training. London: NCET.

National Council of States on In-Service Education, 1976, In-Service Newsletter (May). Syracuse: Syracuse University School of Education.

Parlett, M. and Hamilton, D., 1972, Evaluation as Illumination: A New Approach to the Study of Innovatory Programmes. Edinburgh University: Centre for Research in the Educational Science.

Perry, G. and P., 1969, Case Studies in Teaching. London: Pitman.

Pratt, S. (ed.), 1973, Staff Development in Education. London: Councils and Education Press.

Richardson, E., 1973, The Teacher, The School and the Task of Management. London: Heinemann Educational Books Ltd.

Rogers, E. M. and Shoemaker, F. F., 1971, Communication of Innovations: A Cross-Cultural Approach. London: Collier-Macmillan Ltd.

Schmuck, R. A. and Miles, M., 1971, Organization Development in Schools, National Press Books, Palo Alto, California.

Skilbeck, M., 1976, "School-based curriculum development and teacher education policy", Teachers as Innovators. Paris: OECD.

Smith, E. B., 1975, "Improvement of in-service education: a collaborative effort". In Edelfelt, R. A. and Johnson, M. (eds.), Rethinking In-Service Education. Washington D. C.: National Education Association.

Stake, R. E., 1976, CERI - Evaluating Educational Programmes. Paris: OECD.

Stufflebeam, D. et al., 1971, Educational Evaluation and Decision Making. Itasca, Illinois: F. E. Peacock Publishers Inc.

Taylor, W., 1973, Heading for Change. London: Routledge and Kegan Paul.

Taylor, J. K. and Dale, I. R., 1971, A Survey of Teachers in Their First Year of Service. Bristol: University of Bristol, School of Education.

Vanderpool, J. A., 1975, "Relationships between certification and 'in-service' education". In Edelfelt, R. A. and Johnson, M. (eds.), Rethinking In-Service Education. Washington D. C.: National Education Association.

Warr, P., Bird, M. and Rackham, J., 1970, Evaluation of Management Training. Caver Press.

Waterhouse, P., 1976, Resource-Based Learning in Action. (Pamphlet) Resources for Learning Development Unit, Redcross Street, Bristol, BS2 OBA.

Weiss, C.H., 1972, Evaluation Research - Methods for Assessing Program Effectiveness. Methods of Social Science Series. N.Y. Englewood Cliffs: Prentice Hall Inc.

Yarger, S.J., 1974, A Descriptive Study of the Teacher Center Movement in American Education. Syracuse, New York: Syracuse University.

Appendix 2

THE CASE STUDIES

The pre-seminar national reports contained 35 case studies of innovative approaches to INSET. These ranged widely over many types of approach and institution.

1. The six Australian studies were of the INSET role of the Federal Schools Commission; a regional INSET strategy in Victoria; the Tasmanian Centre for Continuing Education; the Teaching Resources Centre of the Australian Capital Territory; school-based INSET; and the Australian Science Teachers' Education Project.

2. The two Canadian studies were of the PERMAMA Maths project using multimedia methods and the Lighthouse Learning Project at the Atlantic Institute of Education, Halifax.

3. The four French studies were of a centrally initiated INSET programme on innovative teaching methods involving the entitlement to release for all primary teachers; the Maurice Bacquet Physical Education course using action research methods; a research-oriented programme to equip first-cycle secondary teachers with pupil-centred techniques; and a training course in social psychology and group skills.

4. The German and Swiss studies were of a programme related to the introduction of comprehensive schools in West Berlin; a classroom-oriented programme for secondary teachers in Canton Argau involving six months release on full pay; and a programme in Canton Lucerne linking curriculum reform with INSET for handicraft teachers according to a particular theoretical model.

5. The four Japanese studies were of a shceme for overseas visits by teachers; of the fifty-six educational research and training centres throughout the country; of the ways in which school-based research is being stimulated in medium and large size schools; and of a foundation-funded audio-visual aids centre.

6. The four Netherlands studies were of the TELEAC distance-teaching programme to equip teachers for the new flexible schools; a scheme to train counsellors in Utrecht; a foundation-funded programme on creative arts in the primary school; a curriculum development linked programme for mathematics in vocational schools; and an appendix on support centres for teachers.

7. The five Swedish studies were of centrally co-ordinated policy-oriented INSET; study days with locally determined content; study days with centrally determined content; methods of evaluating INSET; and the PLUS project for training educational administrators.

8. The five UK studies (not including Scotland and Northern Ireland) were of the teacher induction pilot schemes project; the new INSET role of Colleges of Education; the Open University; teachers centres and local curriculum development in relation to INSET; and school-based INSET.

9. The two USA reports provided an extensive overview of INSET issues and innovative approaches including the teacher centre movement; staff development in Lincoln, Nebraska; theoretical and survey data collection at Stanford, California; new advisory roles; and the application of competency-based approaches to INSET at Houston, Texas.

10. Finally, a post-seminar contribution from Italy included a study of the OPPI - the Organisation for Teacher Training.

Appendix 3

A PROVISIONAL CONCEPTUAL FRAMEWORK

Throughout the reports and the seminar there were constant pleas for a more rigorous conceptualisation of INSET. This arose partly because of the differing terminology and institutional arrangements in the various countries, but a more fundamental cause was the lack of explicitness in the definition of key concepts and some disagreement about those that were explicit. These difficulties were apparent from the outset of this attempt to review and synthesise the various reports and seminar contributions.

Reviewers of the teacher education literature from within even one country frequently mention the difficulty of deciding upon an appropriate organising framework; the problem for the reviewer of international literature is obviously much more complex still. Moreover, the literature on INSET cannot easily be separated from that on pre-service teacher education, nor, indeed, from work on the training of administrators and other educationists. Ultimately we may need a framework which can encompass the continuing education and training of the education profession in general but that is a daunting task.

Continuing professional development for teachers is a complex enough concept and attempts to give it practical expression in terms of organisational structures and programme contents and methods are correspondingly difficult. In order to simplify the analysis and presentation, this report concentrates primarily on INSET for teachers and makes only passing reference to pre-service education and training (PRESET) and to the training needs of other professional educationists.

The framework used here is a variant on the systems approach (cf. Lomax, 1973). It draws upon innovation theory and applies an innovation process model to the analysis of INSET. In so doing, references are made to works on INSET and educational innovation which were not dealt with in the various country reports or the seminar. This particular theoretical perspective has been expounded elsewhere (Bolam, 1974 and 1976). It distinguishes between the change agent, the innovation and the user. These three factors are defined as open systems, with internal and external or contextual characteristics, which interact with, and are changed by, each other during the course of the innovation process over time.

Figure A1 applies this framework to a diagramatic analysis of the continuing professional development of teachers. Dimension A distinguishes between the major types of providing agency but leaves implicit the notion that each of these "change agents" will have access to a variety of change strategies and communication models or methods. These may be used in relation to the two main task areas distinguished in Dimension B - the formulation of policies and structures and of the content of programmes. Finally, Dimension C distinguishes between the users for whom these strategies, methods and tasks are intended: individual professionals and various types of organisations or systems.

Figure A 1

CONTINUING PROFESSIONAL DEVELOPMENT FOR TEACHERS : AN ANALYTIC FRAMEWORK

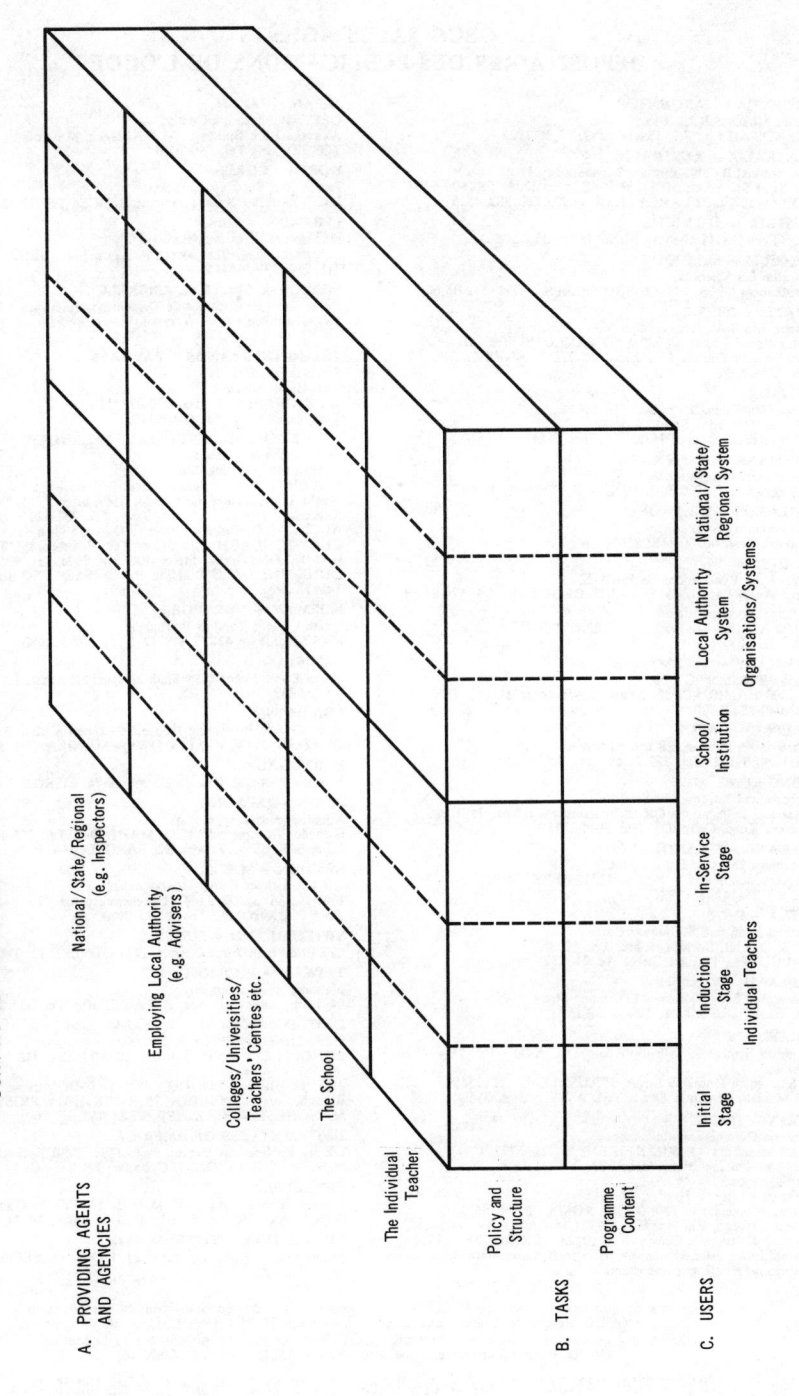

A. PROVIDING AGENTS AND AGENCIES
- National/State/Regional (e.g. Inspectors)
- Employing Local Authority (e.g. Advisers)
- Colleges/Universities/Teachers' Centres etc.
- The School
- The Individual Teacher

B. TASKS
- Policy and Structure
- Programme Content

C. USERS
- Initial Stage
- Induction Stage
- In-Service Stage
- Individual Teachers
- School/Institution
- Local Authority System
- National/State/Regional System
- Organisations/Systems

OECD SALES AGENTS
DÉPOSITAIRES DES PUBLICATIONS DE L'OCDE

ARGENTINA – ARGENTINE
Carlos Hirsch S.R.L., Florida 165,
BUENOS-AIRES, Tel. 33-1787-2391 Y 30-7122

AUSTRALIA – AUSTRALIE
International B.C.N. Library Suppliers Pty Ltd.,
161 Sturt St., South MELBOURNE, Vic. 3205. Tel. 699-6388
P.O.Box 202, COLLAROY, NSW 2097. Tel. 982 4515

AUSTRIA – AUTRICHE
Gerold and Co., Graben 31, WIEN 1. Tel. 52.22.35

BELGIUM – BELGIQUE
Librairie des Sciences,
Coudenberg 76-78, B 1000 BRUXELLES 1. Tel. 512-05-60

BRAZIL – BRÉSIL
Mestre Jou S.A., Rua Guaipà 518,
Caixa Postal 24090, 05089 SAO PAULO 10. Tel. 261-1920
Rua Senador Dantas 19 s/205-6, RIO DE JANEIRO GB.
Tel. 232-07. 32

CANADA
Renouf Publishing Company Limited,
2182 St. Catherine Street West,
MONTREAL, Quebec H3H 1M7 Tel. (514) 937-3519

DENMARK – DANEMARK
Munksgaards Boghandel,
Nørregade 6, 1165 KØBENHAVN K. Tel. (01) 12 69 70

FINLAND – FINLANDE
Akateeminen Kirjakauppa
Keskuskatu 1, 00100 HELSINKI 10. Tel. 625.901

FRANCE
Bureau des Publications de l'OCDE,
2 rue André-Pascal, 75775 PARIS CEDEX 16. Tel. 524.81.67
Principal correspondant :
13602 AIX-EN-PROVENCE : Librairie de l'Université.
Tel. 26.18.08

GERMANY – ALLEMAGNE
Verlag Weltarchiv G.m.b.H.
D 2000 HAMBURG 36, Neuer Jungfernstieg 21.
Tel. 040-35-62-500

GREECE – GRÈCE
Librairie Kauffmann, 28 rue du Stade,
ATHÈNES 132. Tel. 322.21.60

HONG-KONG
Government Information Services,
Sales and Publications Office, Beaconsfield House, 1st floor,
Queen's Road, Central. Tel. H-233191

ICELAND – ISLANDE
Snaebjörn Jónsson and Co., h.f.,
Hafnarstraeti 4 and 9, P.O.B. 1131, REYKJAVIK.
Tel. 13133/14281/11936

INDIA – INDE
Oxford Book and Stationery Co.:
NEW DELHI, Scindia House. Tel. 45896
CALCUTTA, 17 Park Street. Tel.240382

IRELAND - IRLANDE
Eason and Son, 40 Lower O'Connell Street,
P.O.B. 42, DUBLIN 1. Tel. 74 39 35

ISRAËL
Emanuel Brown: 35 Allenby Road, TEL AVIV. Tel. 51049/54082
also at:
9, Shlomzion Hamalka Street, JERUSALEM. Tel. 234807
48, Nahlath Benjamin Street, TEL AVIV. Tel. 53276

ITALY – ITALIE
Libreria Commissionaria Sansoni:
Via Lamarmora 45, 50121 FIRENZE. Tel. 579751
Via Bartolini 29, 20155 MILANO. Tel. 365083
Sub-depositari:
Editrice e Libreria Herder,
Piazza Montecitorio 120, 00 186 ROMA. Tel. 674628
Libreria Hoepli, Via Hoepli 5, 20121 MILANO. Tel. 865446
Libreria Lattes, Via Garibaldi 3, 10122 TORINO. Tel. 519274
La diffusione delle edizioni OCSE è inoltre assicurata dalle migliori librerie nelle città più importanti.

JAPAN – JAPON
OECD Publications Center,
Akasaka Park Building, 2-3-4 Akasaka, Minato-ku,
TOKYO 107. Tel. 586-2016

KOREA - CORÉE
Pan Korea Book Corporation,
P.O.Box n° 101 Kwangwhamun, SÉOUL. Tel. 72-7369

LEBANON – LIBAN
Documenta Scientifica/Redico,
Edison Building, Bliss Street, P.O.Box 5641, BEIRUT.
Tel. 354429–344425

MEXICO & CENTRAL AMERICA
Centro de Publicaciones de Organismos Internacionales S.A.,
Av. Chapultepec 345, Apartado Postal 6-981
MEXICO 6, D.F. Tel. 533-45-09

THE NETHERLANDS – PAYS-BAS
Staatsuitgeverij
Chr. Plantijnstraat
'S-GRAVENHAGE. Tel. 070-814511
Voor bestillingen: Tel. 070-624551

NEW ZEALAND – NOUVELLE-ZÉLANDE
The Publications Manager,
Government Printing Office,
WELLINGTON: Mulgrave Street (Private Bag),
World Trade Centre, Cubacade, Cuba Street,
Rutherford House, Lambton Quay, Tel. 737-320
AUCKLAND: Rutland Street (P.O.Box 5344), Tel. 32.919
CHRISTCHURCH: 130 Oxford Tce (Private Bag), Tel. 50.331
HAMILTON: Barton Street (P.O.Box 857), Tel. 80.103
DUNEDIN: T & G Building, Princes Street (P.O.Box 1104),
Tel. 78.294

NORWAY – NORVÈGE
Johan Grundt Tanums Bokhandel,
Karl Johansgate 41/43, OSLO 1. Tel. 02-332980

PAKISTAN
Mirza Book Agency, 65 Shahrah Quaid-E-Azam, LAHORE 3.
Tel. 66839

PHILIPPINES
R.M. Garcia Publishing House, 903 Quezon Blvd. Ext.,
QUEZON CITY, P.O.Box 1860 – MANILA. Tel. 99.98.47

PORTUGAL
Livraria Portugal, Rua do Carmo 70-74, LISBOA 2. Tel. 360582/3

SPAIN – ESPAGNE
Mundi-Prensa Libros, S.A.
Castelló 37, Apartado 1223, MADRID-1. Tel. 275.46.55
Libreria Bastinos, Pelayo, 52, BARCELONA 1. Tel. 222.06.00

SWEDEN – SUÈDE
AB CE Fritzes Kungl Hovbokhandel,
Box 16 356, S 103 27 STH, Regeringsgatan 12,
DS STOCKHOLM. Tel. 08/23 89 00

SWITZERLAND – SUISSE
Librairie Payot, 6 rue Grenus, 1211 GENÈVE 11. Tel. 022-31.89.50

TAIWAN – FORMOSE
National Book Company,
84-5 Sing Sung Rd., Sec. 3, TAIPEI 107. Tel. 321.0698

UNITED KINGDOM – ROYAUME-UNI
H.M. Stationery Office, P.O.B. 569,
LONDON SEI 9 NH. Tel. 01-928-6977, Ext. 410
or
49 High Holborn, LONDON WC1V 6 HB (personal callers)
Branches at: EDINBURGH, BIRMINGHAM, BRISTOL,
MANCHESTER, CARDIFF, BELFAST.

UNITED STATES OF AMERICA
OECD Publications Center, Suite 1207, 1750 Pennsylvania Ave.,
N.W. WASHINGTON, D.C.20006. Tel. (202)724-1857

VENEZUELA
Libreria del Este, Avda. F. Miranda 52, Edificio Galipán,
CARACAS 106. Tel. 32 23 01/33 26 04/33 24 73

YUGOSLAVIA – YOUGOSLAVIE
Jugoslovenska Knjiga, Terazije 27, P.O.B. 36, BEOGRAD.
Tel. 621-992

Les commandes provenant de pays où l'OCDE n'a pas encore désigné de dépositaire peuvent être adressées à :
OCDE, Bureau des Publications, 2 rue André-Pascal, 75775 PARIS CEDEX 16.
Orders and inquiries from countries where sales agents have not yet been appointed may be sent to:
OECD, Publications Office, 2 rue André-Pascal, 75775 PARIS CEDEX 16.

OECD PUBLICATIONS, 2, rue André-Pascal, 75775 Paris Cedex 16 - No.40.529 1978
PRINTED IN FRANCE